This Book is Dedicated:

To:

_____

From:

_____

The air is poetry,

and I'm trying to grasp His words.

His feelings nimbly fluctuate,

From breeze to bluster.

Poetic air,

He's a sentimental wind.

Passing through me,

I exhale.

And become empty and still.

Where I can hear Him speaking,

In Shapes, Shades and Colors of Me.

Sincerely,
Julia

MyPsalms
Shapes, Shades and Colors of ME

by Julia Su Jack

© 2014 by the author of this book Julia Su. Jack. The book author retains sole copyright to his or her contributions to this book. All artwork is created by Julia Su. Jack.

No part of this book may be reproduced, stored in a retrieval system, or transmitted in any form, or by any means, electronic, mechanical, photonoindenting, recording or otherwiese, without express written consent of the author, except in case of brief excerpts in critical reviews or articles. All inquires should be addressed to WhiteHouse.BrownDoor@gmail.com

ISBN: 978-1-63315-738-5

Printed in the United States

The Blurb-provided layout designs and graphic elements are copyright Blurb Inc., 2014. This book was created using the Blurb creative publishing service. The book author retains sole copyright to his or her contributions to this book.

This Book is Dedicated

To God who gave me the rules of Love,

~~~~~

To My Husband, Joseph,

Who showed me Love in Action,

~~~~~

To my five children

Who taught me how selflessness reverberates,

~~~~~

To My Dad

My active and passive teacher,

~~ and ~~

To my Mom, Maurva,

Without whom I, *on so many levels*,

would simply not be.

CONTENTS

RED..*Love*
- Love Transfusion — pp.11
- I Love Me — pp.12
- Hello Love — pp.13
- I Love You — pp.14
- To Be Love — pp.16

YELLOW..*Spirit*
- Freedom — pp.23
- Icicles — pp.24
- Birth — pp.25
- My Joy — pp.26
- The Veil — pp.28
- Pollen — pp.29

GREY..*Struggle*
- Bulimia — pp.33
- Falling Away — pp.34
- My Pride — pp.36
- To Be — pp.38
- Surrender — pp.41

BLACK..*Anger*
- Would You — pp.45
- Just Because — pp.46
- The After Counselor — pp.47
- Crazy — pp.48
- Invisible — pp.49
- Exhale — pp.50
- Reproducing Broken — pp.52

WHITE..*God*
- Baptism — pp.57
- Inside — pp.58
- Allure — pp.59
- Talking to Myself — pp.60
- Discipleship — pp.64

RED

Love

Love Transfusion

Reach in
To hug my heart
And I'll reach into yours.
Not to steal it, but to know it.
To cradle it's newborn soul.
Not to claim it or to siphon it,
But to see it and to be it.
Reach in to my heart with two hands now.
Do not be afraid.
It is you and you are me.
And I know you're thirsty.
Attach to my soft and tender heart.
Its' purity is your own.
And we shall be one with the other
In this perfect Love Transfusion.

My Psalms; Red

I Love Me

I have fallen in love with myself.
Making love to myself with my own mind,
Turning myself on with my own thoughts.
Kissing myself with my own eyes,
I can feel myself in the bareness of the air.

I hug myself with my own arms,
Knowing what makes me high,
I woo myself with my own joy.
I walk in unison with myself,
Perfectly united with me.

I dance with me inside myself,
Massaged only by my soul.
I whisper adoration to myself,
And in the silence,
I embrace me.

The sun rises and sets on me now.
Self-love flows from my heart,
Streams of my own angelic light.
I am the White Swan,
Seated firmly in God's ocean.

I tenderly cultivate my own essence.
My radiance nurtures me,
And I grow high within my own being.
From the inside to the outside of myself,
I have fallen in love with me.

Hello Love

"Goodbye," my Love.
For I Love you dearly,
But desperately no more.
I let leave of you, Love,
Without conditions.
To fly free like the bird,
Who returns solely,
Upon his own leeward wind.
When love's season calls you,
Back to that eternal,
"Hello," again.

My Psalms; Red

<u>I Love You</u>

From the deepest core of myself
to the outreaches of God and back,
In an ever-begining connected spiral,
I love you.
I love you.
I love you beyond words, beyond language,
    Beyond physical or visual expression,
I love you.
I love you freely, I love you deeply, I love you honestly,
I love you Honorably, I love you fully,
    And inevitably, I love you.
I love you without thought and beyond deed.
I love you.
I love you timeless and forever.
I love you.
I love you silently,
    Peacefully I love you.
I love you joyfully,
    Beautiful I love you.
I love you big.
I love you small.
I love you with or without.
From the tips of the tallest tree,
    To everything that is beyond me, I love you.
I love you.
Gracefully, I love you.
Gently, I love you Hard.
    But, not harmful; I love you
I love you.
I love you as my Mother,
I love you as my Father,
I love you as my Sister and my Brother.

My Psalms; Red

I love you before then and I love you after there.
I love you as he; I love you as she; I love you as it, they, them, us and we.
    I love you as Me.
I love you.
Below the depths of the deepest sea,
I love you.
From between separation of you from me,
I love you.
I love you from outside the field of rite,
    And from inside the walls of wrong.
I love you.
Grounded,
    from within the living center of perfect nothingness.
I LOVE YOU.

My Psalms; Red

To Be Love

I had love,
And like an over protective mother clinging
        desperately to her child's infancy,
    I restricted its' autonomy,
and really had nothing.
I lived with love,
    Like a gigolo,
        in a state of fickle infatuation,
and I received nothing.
Desperately incomplete,
    I have wanted to digress back into love.
        To be reabsorbed,
        back into the comfort, safety and abyss
        of my mother's womb.
    In want, I was ungrateful,
I was nothing.
I could see love through the dense emptiness of space,
    Reveled in others union,
        Married by God,
        married to God, together.
        Holding each other in Gods' sight,
        loving each other with God's might.
    From afar, I stood,
    With a dream,
With nothing.

My Psalms; Red

I taste love every time I overindulge,
    In chocolate and ice cream, in Sin.
        I spread perishable layers,
        over the hole in my heart.
    Unfilled, I stand empty.
Filled with a lot of nothing.
I feel love all the time
    In ephemeral temporal shifts of perspective.
        Like in a drug induced state,
        I shrink to places within,
    In there I lie, I live a lie, and I am the lie.
Left as Nothing,
Completely unjustified.
So you see,
Now, I hunger to Be Love.
    Beyond the conception of love,
    in word or deed;
        Beyond the idea of how love should be,
        Beyond the birth of one who could be,
            that love I envision,
            So I need not strive to be that myself.
    This is deception, not Love,
    Delivering more weight for the world.
More nothing.
I desire to Be Love.
    Beyond writing or dreaming about love.

My Psalms; Red

I desire to Be Love.
    Beyond forging love,
    Beyond the giving or taking of love.
    Closer than the momentary emotional bursts
        of fellowship,
            outside of pretense and pretending,
            surpassing the truth to kill the lie,
            free from this earth,
            away from the gravity of purgatory,
    Like before the flicker of the concept of man,
    It was complete and pure,
        undivided and uncorrupted.
I desire to be that Love.
Do not misunderstand,
I do want to possess greater gifts from this world.
I do pray to have a love to protect me.
I want to live with love in a holy union.
I want to be absorbed into love's perfect moments.
I want to see love both inside and outside of myself.
I want to taste love through my body's nourishment.
I want to feel love in all of God's unduplicatable ways.
I want to conceive love's ideas born through thought and deed.
I want to write about it.
I want to dream about it.
I want to forge it, give and receive it.
But, even more that all of theses,

My Psalms; Red

I want,
I desire,
To Be Love,
For without this,
    all of those,
    are temporary,
To Nothing.
I desire to Be Love,
    never, ever again to need it.
    But have it anyway,
        always there,
        like water when I thirst,
        an eternal, internal spring.
  Like living water from the nucleus of God,
I want to liquefy myself to Be That.
So, when I saw Love,
    I picked it up and I took it home.
        Opening my Bible I ate Love,
        and, it transformed me.
Yet, Love still waits for my surrender.
    For me to pause and digest.
        So that through my veins,
            He, the almighty, can take over me.
    Fulfilling the greatest desire of my heart,
    the greatest desire of His heart.
For me
To Be Love.
So that even if I have Nothing,
    I would always have Everything.

Yellow *Spirit*

My Psalms; Yellow

<u>Freedom</u>

Freedom to fly in my own mind.
Freedom to stay locked inside.
Flowing with the waves of any tide.
Blowing by the winds of my Spirits pride.

Freedom to repeat the songs of unknown Nations,
To take the time and to have the patience.
To rock like a swing in repetition,
Repeating,
With continued adulation.

unfleeting-ly,

Free.

To fly in my own mind,
or stay locked inside.
Flowing with the waves of any tide.
Blowing on the winds,
Down my Spirits slide.

My Psalms; Yellow

<u>Icicles</u>

Icicles in suspended animation.
Stopped in movement by an unseen force.
Molded by a spontaneous invocation to halt.
Showing us, as we move in minutes passing,
The vision of the last moment we forgot,
Un-reclaimable.

Icicles in suspended animation
Stopped in movement,
With the potential to pierce,
Into something or someone
After a duration,
Time passes,
Promise undelivered.

As the Icicles in suspended animation,
Cry in the warmth of sister sun,
As she radiates vitamins through her relation,
Reflecting the impermanence of all things.
Icicles in suspended animation,

Stopped with movement, slowly changing.
To feed the forces of colored new birth,
Yet unseen forestation.
To slow us into each moment in time,
Into awareness.
Stopping us to see the miraculous.
Icicles, in suspended animation.

__Birth__

I knocked my soul's head on my way down,
    out into this world.
Through the birth canal I was born,
    in an amnesic state of awareness.
I am a light body in vitro.
    Birthed, yet unborn, yet living still.
I have forgotten from where I have just come.
    Yet, I can recall the palatial feel of the one.
Naked, I have come into this place,
    of cold breezes and cold hearts.
I would turn back,
    but that power is not mine.
So, I declare to speak of this truth.
    but that power is not mine.
Gagged,
    my heart similarly contracts,
        splitting my light, I remain only in part.
That time will come when I again will seek the flame.
    and my living heart will grow twice impassioned.
Then, I shall be born again,
    wholly aware,
        birthed, born, and alive.
Where I will make my start,
    back to live and be alive,
        at the beginning.

My Psalms; Yellow

<u>My Joy</u>

The world stood at my door, with a smile and a box.
A Masked smirk,
Magnetic eyes,
It had a shiny bow.
Yeah I opened it, like you opened it!
And it spit on me…
I wilted, like you wilted!
But, now, I am a Soldieress,
I will not bend, I will not compromise, I will not break.

So, Slice me with your eyes - *and my Joy remains.*
Cut me with your lies - *and my Joy remains.*
Pull me down - *and my Joy lifts me.*
Push me - *and my Joy keeps me standing.*
Harass me and I surrender
    - *As my Joy stands silently to be your mirror.*
Persecute me and I do not wane - *My Joy expands me.*
Intimidate me - *and my Joy stands straight and strong.*
Harm me - *and I remain clean and cleansed by my Joy.*
Spit your pain on me,
    I remain untouched,
        Nothing can penetrate my Joy.
Regurgitate the darkness,
planted from birth in your consciousness.
    I will hold the bucket for you
        My Joy sanitizes me.

Taunt me - *and my Joy applauds.*
Tease me - *and my Joy pays tribute.*
Mock me - *and my Joy is justified.*

My Psalms; Yellow

Do to me the undoable,
    the unnatural,
    the unfair,
    and unfathomable,
        - And my Joy intensifies -
Faithfully my Joy remains -
    Stands firm, faultless and convicted,
My Joy is where darkness is cleansed.
God's electricity energizes my Joy..
Take from me - *and my Joy gives me more*
Lead me astray - *and my Joy finds me and guides me.*
Do what you will,
Because my Joy engulfs me,
    Anesthetizes me to negativity,
        Freeing me from the need.

Darkness is standing before me, with a smile and a box
A Masked smirk,
With a shiny bow
It is not a Gift
And you cannot reach me.
Because now,
I AM JOY.

My Psalms; Yellow

The Veil

...And the veil falls behind my eyes,
In front of my soul,
and I can't see truth.
Disconnected from my self,
in static mis-communication,
I walk with God.
Tormented there by the haze.
It causes me not to see Him clear.
It's payment for release,
The tax for liberation.
But, I am being seasoned,
To be the meat for evolutions last supper.
Led into the tub of fire,
To burn away germs of lifetimes amiss.
Washing first the outer skin,
Then my soul,
Caked with pain's residue.
It is excruciating release,
To become the nourishment for man's journey home.
Calibrating my eyes to comprehend God's grace,
The veil falls.
And....I bathe in the anguish,
Where God's presence is vague.
With that veil behind my eyes,
before my soul it sits,
to be seen and known,
so to not be there anymore.

My Psalms; Yellow

Pollen

Summer snow drifts by,
    as I hear hymns of Jesus,
        I think of you.
The window your eyes.
In them I see it all,
As Summer snow drifts by.

Summer snow drifts by,
    with thoughts of Christmas all year.
And I think of you.
The trees your thighs,
    the windows your eyes.
In them,
Summer snow drifts by.

As if in slow motion,
    tending a child's prayer,
Summer snow drifts by,
And I see it all in your eyes.

As songs of praise take hold.
The leaves your hair.
The grass your skin.
I feel through your eyes.
Drifting by,
    the blue sky in your eyes.
Summer snow,
    and it calms me.

Grey

Struggle

My Psalms; Grey

<u>Bulimia</u>

Food is my medication, my tranquilizer,
    sedative to this dense world.
Desperate to connect with God,
    I overindulge in times of despair, to reach him.
False injections of his ultimate truth into my blood stream,
    Anesthetizing me to this everlastingly dense world.
My crack cocaine, ice creamy illusion of God's fullness.
Ephemeral distraction drives my craving.
So, I scold my wickedness with starvation.
Denying me any association.
Unplugged from Him,
    I suspend my own medication,
    Put myself out naked,
    Causing inner withdrawal and agitation,
    And feel ultimate separation.
It's excruciating.
Contracting from my creator.
Proving no point at all.
    Yet learning, hopefully,
    The lesson,
    Of compassion.
The soprano of God's life energy wefts naturally,
    In and out of my body.
    In every moment of my existence.
Yet still,
I neglect myself to get closer to Him?
    To be higher than Him?
Completely incomplete.
    What dishonor I bring unto earth's womb,
As I desperately attempt to shrink and fade,
    Forever,
    From this debilitating foreign land.

My Psalms; Grey

<u>Falling Away</u>

I am having a hard time,
Unlike a*ny* time before,
I'm just not able to anymore.
To *stretch* myself from the inside out,
To be the one who shades the doubt,
Putting **myself** in the way,
…To save the day.
Stuffing what's outside in,
Just to begin…
To clean the waste,
To clear someone else's spiritual case.
Standing before the judge, unlike before…
I can't do it anymore.
I know **You** did.
Stretched yourself and died for all sin.
But, I am furthest from your kin.
And **You** ask me to bring outsiders in?
To share with those in difficult places.
I used to be able to look into their faces,
To uncover **your** expression…
To help them with passion…
But, I don't have anything to say,
Nothing positive, anyway.
But…
"Welcome to **my** world of pain!"
"Stop whining about **your** rain!"
"Where were you when **my** life unwrapped?"

My Psalms; Grey

"I too am trapped!"…
I'm having a hard time stretching **my self.**
I know the consequence is,
My spiritual health.
In its entirety.
I know you stretched out to death,
Individually.
Beyond this box of self pity.
Labeled, "What About Me."
It is lonely.
It won't let me be free…
I **know** your kingdom is in heaven.
I **know** you are the place to heal.
But not until death do we congeal?
I just can't kneel,
To find the door,
To pull myself out.
Unlike before,
I just can't do it anymore…

My Psalms; Grey

MY_PRIDE

The devil is clothed in the coat of my pride,
    speaking to me from the dark recesses of my mind.
He wears me.
He weights me down.
The heavy material of his hatred
    draws me away from the light.

The devil is clothed in the coat of my pride,
    speaking to me from the dark recesses of my own mind.
He whispers sweet nothingness,
    emptied of all nutrition,
    fattening me up to not fit in God's size.
He distracts me from the melody of God's play,
    telling me tales of easy roads and gentle, slippery ways,

The devil is clothed in the coat of my own pride,
    speaking to me from the dark recesses of my own mind.
I feel "better than" through his simulated skin.
I think I'm "smarter than" through his muddled mind.
I think I deserve "more than" by his false measure.
I think I see "greater vision" through his tinted shades.
I think I speak "clearer than" through his voluminous
voice.

Deception, Deceit, Delusion.

With the devil clothed in the coat of my pride,
    I think it not mine, yet own it still.

My Psalms; Grey

When he speaks to me from the dark recesses of my mind,
   I hear my own voice in voiceless lies speaking to me,
      Yet, I believe them still.

Lies Registered through intense life pain.
Father God!
   "Hallowed be thy name,
   Thy kingdom come
   Thy will be done..."

He is clothed in the coat of my pride,
   Speaking to me from within my own mind.

Rip his skin, my coat of his back.
Expose him naked in his deception.
"Burn him, Blast him,"
"Baste me, Bake me, Refine me, Refresh me!"

...And through Baptism to freedom,
   I heard the silent intimations of God.

My Psalms; Grey

To Be

"Why does the caged bird sing?"
"Why does the caged bird sing?"
"Why does the caged bird sing?"
"Why does the caged bird sing?"

"Why does the caged bird sing?" You ask.

Because I am closed in from my natural way,
    grounded for you to amuse,
        abused for you to care only for yourself.

"Why does the caged bird sing?" They ask.

To be released.
I sing for you to release me.

"Why does the caged bird sing," You ask?

So you may know my true nature and let me be Free!

"Why does the caged bird sing?"

So you may no longer force my grace into a small cage,
    A size convenient only for your house.
    Putting me where I was never meant to be.
    Making me live where I do not belong.

"Why does the caged bird sing?"

Because I am trapped and it's all I've got left.
My therapy, to release the ever-growing,
continually cycling pain of capture.

"Why does the caged bird sing?"

I sing to drown myself in the dreamy illusion of freedom.
I sing because I can not fly.
I am clipped.
No longer able to reach the heights where the breath of God resides.

My Psalms; Grey

Through the veil of time where my sisters and bothers watch the angels dancing.
Free...

"Why does the caged bird sing?"

I scream a mantra to God
    to drown out the vision of the bars holding me.
        Trapped, enwrapped, held in, tied down.
Beautiful scrams of pain calling God!
    For you to release me.

"Why does the caged bird sing?"

To throw myself into trance
    Back into my natural state of soaring
    Like in a dream
    Back up with the eagles and doves, ravens and red breasts

---

"Why do I sing?"

I sing sour sorrow
    of my inevitable recapture
    now the only gift of consciousness.

"Why does the caged bird sing?"

Because I can not cry wet tears from my eyes,
    I cry tears through my mouth
    In notes and tones forming pools of melodies
    For you to release me.

I understand the perfection of God's plan,
    But, stand paralyzed in question
    Why,
    Have I been captured?

"Why do I sing?"

To get you to hear.
For you to see,
That I am unwillingly trapped.
Mistreated, you are keeping me,

My Psalms; Grey

Caring or me, only for yourself.

"Why do I sing?"

This indentured servant sings in payment for her freedom.
    In hopes of one day owning her own land,
    Freedom,
        To liberate other caged and unwillingly tamed hearts.

I am God's bird.
Hear my prayer.
And set me Free.

"Why does the caged bird sing," You ask still?

Don't you hear me?
I cry pools of tears
    Songs beyond this time
    Just to pass, if only in my mind,
    Through the bars of your sin,
    To dine on imaginary worms from God's table.

I sing because you can't see me.

"Why does the caged bird sing?"

"To be, or Not to Be?"
That is the question.

My Psalms; Grey

SURRENDER

YOU ARE TIRED AND WEARY,
THE BUMPS IN THE ROAD, THE GAP IN YOUR PATH TO EVERLASTING LIFE SEEM TO BE INCREASING.

GET UP.
DO NOT SIT DOWN, BUT SURRENDER.
YOU'RE NAVIGATING WITH THE WRONG INSTRUMENT, YOUR COMPASS IS AMISS.

LISTEN NOW NOT TO YOUR RADIOS' CONFUSED TUNING
BUT, TO THAT DISTANT CALLING OF SPIRIT'S DIRECTION

STAND UP AND SURRENDER.
THE ILLUSION HAS GOT YOU RUNNING IN PLACE.

Would You

If I lost my mind,
Would you know?
Would you care?

If I go astray,
Would you be there?

If I lost my sight,
Would you see?
Would you narrate the world to me?

Or would you sit in your excuse of blindness?
Remain numb and mindless.

If I misplaced it,
Would you find it?

If you forget me,
Would you be reminded?

My Psalms; Black

<u>Just Because</u>

Just because I seem not be able to,
Don't exclude me.
Just because.
Just because I seem not to have time to,
Don't neglect to ask me.
Just because.
Just because I seem far away from,
Don't leave me out.
Just because.
Just because I seem different than,
Don't avoid me.
Just because.
Just because I seem not to have enough of,
Don't go without me.
Just because.
Just because I seem not to want to,
Don't overlook me.
Just because.
Just because I seem not ready for,
Don't assume I can't.
Just because.
Just because I seem not to see,
Don't pretend I'm not there.
Just because.
Just because?
Just because it hurts me.

My Psalms; Black

<u>The After Counselor</u>

Joy is not what swung by in the Camaro,
      and picked you up off the front porch last night.
Happy is not what coaxed you,
      to sneak out of your dorm window, right?
Fun is not what got you drinking the beer,
      that ignited the fight.
Excitement is not what drove that car off the highway,
      into the construction site.
and Love is not what ended your life,
That was a Man and his mental was not right.

My Psalms; Black

Crazy

I live in the belly of darkness,
    the underbelly of sin,
        talking with the devil within.
The valley of the shadow of death,
    lurks at my bedroom door.
The devil is stalking me.
"Dark one, No More!"
"Can I live in the time, where sin-free ways reign?"
"Not in the underbelly where you remain."
"Here where sinful dress retains,
    it's whole, uncut form."
"Alterable by hope?"
"Will I will be the free imprisoned slave?"
I live in the belly of darkness,
    in sin-filled pain.
The underbelly of the devil,
    and his trashy evil ways.
In the landfill of darkness,
    is where I spend my days.
        after day,
    and nights,
I live in the underbelly of the darkest sin,
    conversing crazy with the devil within.

<u>Invisible</u>

If I stood before you naked,
    would you see me?

If I give myself to you,
    would you honor me?

Sipping me like fine wine,
    would you savor me?
Or would I be cold beer guzzled on a high hot day?
    wasted like long left milk,
        poured down the drain into the abyss?

Would you rub me with the silver polish of your affection?

Cherish and covet me like a rare coin?

Or would I be the foreign currency in your foreign terrain?

If you pressed your palm to the center of me,
    you would feel my longing,
        and no longer deny me your affection.

Could I be your jewel?

Can I be your friend?

Am I anything to you at all?

I am standing completely naked in front of you.

Do you even see me?

My Psalms; Black

Exhale

I was a loyal wife.

-INHALE-

I closed my mouth.
I plugged my nose.

-INHALE-

I held my breath and
Was punched with my insecurities.
Anger blasted inward.

-INHALE-

Holding my breath,
I was socked with your self-hate and
Inward blasted disdain.

-INHALE-

Holding my breath, long and dedicatedly
You hit me with my dependence and
In went self-loathing.

-INHALE-

Holding my breath, deep and full now
You jumped on me with false loyalty and
I vomited pain inside myself.

-INHALE-

My Psalms; Black

Holding my breath,
You smacked me with your own self destruction.
And spawned rage inside me.

I continued to hold my breath
and -INHALED- even more.

But, you made a mistake...

-INHALE-

Holding my breath for the last time.
You surrounded me with your enormity,
I EXHALED,
And your life Exploded.

My Psalms; Black

REPRODUCING BROKEN

A broken man gifted to me poverty
Blinded by spiritual paucity
He fed my naivety
And emptiness consumed me
Ingesting someone else's pain blindly
I became angry

That anger skulked up to agony
Spreading injuriously
As youthfulness sacredly
Justified my indignity
In a mask of advocacy
As his inner demon giftedly
Strangled me
Internally

My life progressed this way instinctively
But, I sickened of deficiency
Of courting greatness failingly
I got tired falling repeatedly
Loosing relations due to fluency
With the language of spiritual miscarriage that vividly
Outwardly
Was defining me

My God in birth duplicated me
And I was able to see clearly
The unfailing delivery
From him through me cursorily
To her, finally
The transcendental poverty
Ready to capture a new detainee

My Psalms; Black

In an amplified spiritual expiry
Butchery
Through naivety
To anger
Agony
And indignity

I stood up and finally
Disowned it psychologically
The legacy strangling our eternity
To a new internal advocacy
A spiritual reality
Because now I could see our destiny
Through the video fatally
Playing behind my eyes continually
And I wouldn't go back to living violently
A pain someone else wanted to giftedly
Turn on me
From his generationally
Conveyed legacy
Of inadequacy.

White

God

My Psalms; White

Baptism

Today my heart sings to birth my soul.

God's reverberating harmonies sing clear light through me.
No longer does my heart sing to me songs of sorrow in wrongdoing

And I listen now.

Not in protocol,
For obligations sake.
Nor to follow the bible's ruling.
But, because my heart sings to me God's harmony,
A melody of clear light straight through me.

And I listen.

Submerge with me into the luminous depths,
Emerging with our souls forever interconnected,
Surrendered in trust.
God will reveal there truth to us,
Love will radiate from us,
Enveloped in the truth of heaven.

Listen.

Sing to me, Father, your melodies,
Golden, radiant liquid harmony,
And surround me with your living water,
Bound in your silent spell of rapture.

My Psalms; White

Inside

God lives inside whispering truth to you
    in the silent recesses of your mind.
Telling you to retreat from your eyes
    back through his, to see perfection.
God lives inside to speak through you,
    bidding you speak truth and ungag Him.
Living inside for you to hear.
Listen to the sweet aroma of light
    that filters through His heart.
He lives inside to touch you,
    so you may know your perfect place.
God lives inside with the present of truth,
    wrapped and waiting to gift to you.
He lives inside wanting, just waiting,
    for you to turn inward to Him
        and reach out your hand.

Allure

The smell of fresh baked dough in the morning.
Alluring, after a night's sleep fasting.
God feels like that.
That smell pulling you,
Dragging you craving,
To desire's need.
God,
Like the rush of slightly melted ice cream,
Sweet, sliding over the tong.
Desiring ever more,
God,
In every moment of my existence.
Emerging from the shade,
God draws me into the the light,
Warmth wrapping,
Peacefully holding,
Contentment enveloping.
God,
The mother of all.
Resting my head on her soft chest,
Bearing slumber.
The Father of all,
I have to sink into him.
Like the Angelic kiss,
Moist and gentle,
From love's guardian heart,
The truth of God re-awakens me.

My Psalms; White

Talking to Myself

What if God is inside you?

What if when you feel,
Someone else made you to…
You self-respond,
From that all powerful source,
That is not beyond,
But inside you.

What if God is inside you?

What if you're intended to promenade
In constant fog, trusting God
With each and every step,
Your every direction.
To see every stumble,
Not as an ultimate correction
But a private hint.
From inside you.

What if God is inside you?

What if I take it humbly
When you obviously don't love me
And instead of wastefully weeping
I trust my own heart
Gracefully in self-keeping
To the one that is
Inside me.

What if God is inside me?

My Psalms; White

What if our separation
Is only a physical affirmation
Of the simple fact
That I have your back
Because we are ultimately connected
And on track
With the One "I Am,"
Inside Us.

What if God is inside us?

What if when they gather
We don't see a gang but rather
A bunch of wounded souls
Feeling dejected
People, beings, consciousness unknowingly
Attached and protected
To the One "I Am"
Inside *Us*.

What if God is not anonymous,
But is realistically, genuinely, faithfully
The One "I Am,"
Alive inside us?...

What if instead of making myself dirty
Remembering everything that hurt me
I abandoned that contemplation
Not as an internal accommodation
But, to a shelf outside myself
For total forgiveness
From inside me.

What if God is inside me?

My Psalms; White

What if like the sundial
You stand straight
And just wait…
For God's light to illustrate,
The right direction
So others too, can make the correction
To find the One "I Am,"
Inside them.

What if God is inside you?

Like breath to an empty lung,
What if you give life to my compassion.
Forgetting my faults, you happen
To convey the living energy
Through me
Proving to actually Be
The One "I Am"
Inside Me.

Would you see yourself differently?…

What if God is actually inside you?

What if God is not restricted
To this humanly devised district
Outside the surface of your skin
But penetrates from without to within
And with singlehanded plurality
Is the great, "I Am"
Inside you, Inside me.

What if God is inside me?

My Psalms; White

What if when I seek God's guiding tempo individually,
He gives pace to our hearts collectively?

What if when I meditate independently
You can perceive me,
Audibly.

What if,
I'm just talking to myself...

My Psalms; White

<u>Discipleship</u>

God precedes your entrance,
    and it's the sweet scent of Jesus that lingers
    when you leave.
you are God's sweet disease infecting my dream,
    sweeping all darkness away,
    laying down sheets of clear light in your wake.
you are God's angel showering blooming ashes of Love
    up, down, over, around and onto my hell's fire
you are God's speaker here to sing me clear,
    to take root in me,
        plugging in to the diving,
        you blast waves of force through me,
            power tones from God's electric guitar.
you are God's hunger i crave,
    to nourish my-self,
        i feed from your infinite soul source.
as God's channel,
    you are here to tune me in,
        to lead me home,
            to Him who is the one who proceeded your coming,
            and who will leave lingering
                the sweet scent of Jesus
                    when you are gone.

blurb